Los Angeles.
During its 20 the city has drawn in waves of p something special. From cattle an screen, the West Coast metropoli dangled the hope of making the impossible possible.

The sundrenched vision of Venice Beach rollerbladers and Hollywood starlets has been ruptured in past decades by tensions of poverty and racial division. Now, middle-class people are flooding into former ganglands, as an electric fusion of cultures takes place.

Yet that's always been the way with Los Angeles— the pressure to succeed versus easy living, darkness jostling the light... Meanwhile, the constantly shifting sprawl remains at the forefront of cuisine, music and the arts.

In the end it's the people who shape the feel of a city. In Los Angeles we spoke to gifted personalities: a hip-hop legend and music producer, a filmmaker and actress, a fashion designer and artist couple, a food expert and a beach-side family. Our picks are complemented by a feature story, a photo showcase and flash fiction, from global and local talents. It's all about original minds and the creative vibe. Get lost in the sights, smells and flavours of the city. Get lost in Los Angeles.

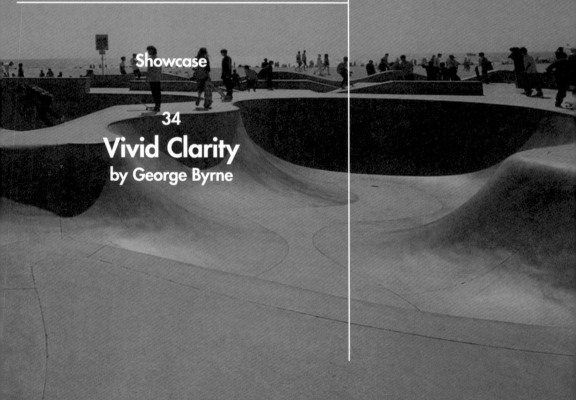

The post-apocalyptic concrete basin of the Los Angeles River has been seen in countless movies from "Grease" to "Terminator 2". And, as with everything else in LA, it has flowed a chequered course through poor urban planning, uprooted communities and real estate shenanigans. The channel was poured with concrete in the late 1930s to stop floods engulfing the city, obliterating the life-giving

water flow that attracted the first settlers. Local campaigners and artists have worked to revitalise it for decades, but it's a controversial development plan involving the city mayor and mega architect Frank Gehry that's shaping up to be one of the biggest makeovers in the city's history.

Funny Bones

Are you having a laugh? At the UCB you're bound to. The *Upright Citizen Brigade* is a seething cesspool of comedic talent. From Amy Poehler to Aziz Ansari, the list of big-name comedians who have learned and perfected their craft there is as long as the Pacific Rim. Stand-up, improv, variety and a fair share of "fits no label" weird stuff—whatever you might crave, artistic director Mike Stills' brigade serves it up. And when you get home—one of the comedians you just saw might well have a new series on Netflix.
• UCB Theatre, Hollywood, ucbtheatre.com

From Mayan Mansions to Sci-Fi Trails

Anything is Possible

Outdoor **Endless Summer**

The Venice and Santa Monica shore may deliver the most iconic LA ocean views but there is more to explore: Head to *Manhattan Beach* (pictured) and *Hermosa Beach* for an urban vibe. Wave riders should opt for Malibu's *Zuma* or *Surfrider Beach*. Some miles further up the Pacific Coast Highway, *Leo Carrillo* and *El Matador Beach* offer pure nature with boulders and sea caves. The perfect spots to watch the sun going down with a glass of Californian white wine are *Paradise Cove* or *Topanga State Beach*—at least on less crowded weekdays.
• Various locations, see Index p.63

Old School Flavours

A lot of LA places claim to be the originators or the best in town at whatever they're dishing up. But few are the real deal. *Bill's Burgers* in Van Nuys however, does have credentials with its American double cheese burger. So dedicated to the patty is Bill that he still uses his 1930s grill, and doesn't waste time perfecting fries—here, a bag of Lay's potato crisps and a frosty PBR beer are the go-to sides. At *Langer's Deli* in Westlake the top recommendation is the iconic #19 pastrami sandwich. Langer's invented it, and their hours-steamed pastrami has arguably been best in the business since 1947. If you want to do breakfast, lunch or late-night shakes at a legitimate American diner, hit the *101 Coffee Shop* in Hollywood's Best Western. It has a loyal patronage and has been a landmark for decades—you might even remember its role in "Swingers". A careful restoration in 2001 preserved its 1960s charm and fantastic jukebox. Also in the Best Western is *MiniBar*, a refined, slick-looking hangout that'll make you feel like you're waiting for Don Draper to order you an Old Fashioned.

• Various locations, see Index p.63

Movie Palace

Return to the golden age of the silver screen at *Theater at Ace Hotel*. The staggering auditorium in the gothic style is dripping with luscious details, belying its inspiration in Spain's 16th-century Segovia Cathedral. Mary Pickford, Douglas Fairbanks and Charlie Chaplin all turned out for its opening in 1927. The crowd might be a little different since its restoration by Ace, but the space has lost none of its majesty. Book ahead for events including the occasional silent movie with live accompaniment.
• Theater at Ace Hotel, Downtown, acehotel.com

Outdoor | **Space Walking**

Among the traffic-clogged city's secrets are its various hiking trails, taking you up through surrounding hills and rewarding the adventurous with bird's-eye views. *Vasquez Rocks* will delight nature lovers as much as movie buffs. The park offers trails suited to various thigh capacities and a stunning, otherworldly landscape that has been the backdrop for productions like "Star Trek" and "The Flintstones". Come early, bring water and be prepared to encounter the occasional superfan on a pilgrimage.
• Vasquez Rocks Natural Area Park, Agua Dulce

10

Culture **Mayan Masterpiece**

Drink in a panoramic view of Hollywood from the summit of this Los Feliz hilltop, then feast your senses on the Frank Lloyd Wright masterpiece of *Hollyhock House*. Built in 1921 as an arts centre for an eccentric oil heiress, flooding and other issues meant she couldn't live in it herself. But what it lacks in practicality it makes up for aesthetically—with the majestic presence of a Mayan temple. It's worth taking a tour for more info—then finding the *Los Angeles Municipal Art Gallery*, located nearby in the same green space of Barnsdall Art Park.
• Hollyhock House, Barnsdall Art Park, East Hollywood, barnsdall.org

Food **Hitting the Lottery**

It's infamously difficult to secure a table at Curtis Stones' 25-seat restaurant *Maude*. One reason is the Australian chef's celebrity status—he's touted as the Antipodean rivalled in fame only by Russell Crowe. Book well ahead to eat here via their online ticket system, however, and you'll realise the fame is only half the story—because *Maude* is all about the food. One vegetable ingredient is the star each month, and foundation to each of the nine courses in your meal. That means if you do land a table, you could end up testing the limits of the black truffle—or the humble radish.
• Maude, Beverly Hills, mauderestaurant.com

Chris Manak
He started off selling mixtapes at school before making his name as a true talent of 1990s hip hop. When his partner MC Charizma was killed he turned to instrumental work, riding the rise of the solo DJ. In 1996 he founded Stones Throw Records; the first record was a tribute to his late friend. In recent years Peanut Butter Wolf has mostly been touring, promoting acts like Madlib and spotting the stars of tomorrow

Chris Manak aka Peanut Butter Wolf, DJ & Producer

Cross Cutting

The DJ, producer and label manager tells us about his work and his multi-faceted town, pointing out spots to dance with hot newcomers, where to grab tasty fish tacos and how to find the Santa Monica pigeon man

You're from San Jose. How did you end up in Los Angeles?

I was 25 years old when I moved from San Jose to San Francisco for a few years because of the hip hop and club scene, and I started my label Stones Throw there. But as a kid I always wanted to live in LA. As a kid you think of Disneyland and all the movie and music stuff going on, and the beaches and the cute girls, and a lot of my favourite rappers were in LA. When I did move here in 2001 it was more for the music scene and the fact that one of our biggest Stones Throw artists Madlib lives here. But I was welcomed so nicely by the LA community that I just saw myself wanting to try it out at least once.

Is the music scene still as vibrant as when you moved?

Sure. There are always things to do. There is Dâm-Funk's "Funk-mosphere" party, one of the longest running weeklies in LA. It's at *The Virgil*, which is booked by Novena Carmel, the daughter of Sly from Sly & The Family Stone. I definite-ly recommend it for everybody who comes into town. Also Low End Theory at *The Airliner* is still going strong. But there's lots of smaller bars that play good music as well, like *General Lee* and *Melody Lounge*, both in Chinatown, and *Footsies* in Highland Park if you want some-thing more low key. The *Del Monte Speakeasy* in Venice has good music curation too. J. Rocc does parties there. The *Echo/Echoplex* has good music including probably the best weekly reggae party outside of Jamaica called Dub Club. A lot of the hotels have good music too. *The Ace Hotel* in Downtown and the *The Line Hotel* in Koreatown are usually safe bets. For people who do not know LA: if you live on the Eastside, you go out on the East-side. And when you live on

the West you go out in the West, because the traffic here is really a nightmare.

So LA folks stick to their district.

More or less. I am based in Highland Park and as I live here I can't tell you so much about Beverly Hills or West Hollywood. When I moved here 15 years ago everybody was talking about Silver Lake and Echo Park and how it was kind of an artistic community. I couldn't afford it at the time, as I need a big space because of my record collection. So I went a little bit further Northeast where you have Mount Washington, Highland Park and Montecito Heights. Now you have this big artist community here, too.

What is something you look forward to when you come home to your district after playing around the world?

Well, the weather in the first place as it's always warm. And the area I live in (Highland Park) has a lot of used record stores so I'm usually entertaining out-of-towners and taking them record shopping. A lot of the record stores in Highland Park are specialised. Between *Per-manent*, *Wombleton*, *Gimmie Gimmie*, and *Mount Analog*, there's some-thing for everyone. I think Highland Park has the most record stores in LA per square mile.

Anything else in the area that's off the beaten track?

There is *Ernest R. Debs Regional Park* in Montecito Heights—kind of a lesser-known place. It's a few miles northeast of Downtown LA and yet definitely feels like a getaway from city life. It has good trails for hiking and there's a small lake at the top of the mountain. *Echo Park Lake* is also good for recreation. They have paddle boats in the lake and lots of joggers and

Crazy cocktails and bipolar sound at Chinatown's General Lee's: live jazz on the top floor, DJs down below

dog walkers walking around the lake.

Where's good to eat after the walk?
My district has a lot of Mexican restaurants so that's what I eat most. *Via-Mar* serves tasty fish and shrimp tacos. It's not really healthy eating, but it is my guilty pleasure and fun to try if you're not from LA. It's an outdoor covered patio —no indoors seating. Then there's a place called *La Abeja*, which isn't much to look at, but the food is really good. It's been around since the 1960s and it's a typical, simple LA Mexican restaurant. I usually try to take out-of-towners to Mexican restaurants because it's hard to find authentic ones in Europe or Asia or Australia or even on the East Coast of the US! But there's Little Tokyo and Chinatown nearby where you can also eat well too. I think LA has more sushi restaurants than Tokyo. But it depends what kind of food you want to eat. There's a place called *Masa of Echo Park* that has really good pizza. But pizza is really an NY thing to do—the LA thing is to eat a burger and there's nothing more LA than *In-N-Out*. It's been around since I think 1949 and is still independently owned. It's fast food, but much fresher and healthier than the big chains. Just expect to wait in a long line!

What are your favourite beaches in LA?
The beach not far from LA airport is nice. The Westside has nice beaches. I lived for a while in Playa Del Rey, so people go there

Not just a pretty façade: the Line Hotel also is a safe bet for music, according to Peanut Butter Wolf

or Marina Del Rey for a quieter beach or Malibu. If you want more action, there's Santa Monica or Venice Beach. The 3rd Street Promenade in Santa Monica has cool street musicians and there's an old man with a really long beard who has 30-40 pigeons all over him. I do not know how he does it, but it is kind of fun to watch. He moves very slowly. The Mayer Hawthorne video we shot for "Maybe So, Maybe No" had some Venice Beach action.

And what would you advise someone in town just for the weekend?

Well there are places like the *Rose Bowl*, which has one of the world's largest vintage flea markets, monthly on a Sunday. You can find clothes from all decades there. Also knick-

knacks, furniture and other stuff. And if you are in Highland Park, you can go to York Boulevard, a street with a lot of cute stores and restaurants. It's an area people outside of LA do not know really well. There is also Atwater Village close to Griffith Park, which is nice for a day. It really depends on what you're looking for. Some people love going to Rodeo Drive, but I don't think I've ever been.

Where do you go for shopping?

For men's clothes there's a place downtown called *Tanner Goods*. They have tasteful stuff. *Apolis* in the Arts District has good stuff, but I dress pretty conservative. Twentysomethings usually go to mid-Wilshire. They have Supreme, Undefeated, Union, etc. That's where you go if you want to dress like Odd Future. And my girl-friend goes to the Fashion District on Saturday mornings and spends about $100 on like ten outfits.

LA has many museums, but which ones are special?

Everybody is talking about *The Broad*, which is new. But I have not been there yet as the lines are crazy right now. They feature new, contemporary stuff. And the *Natural History Museum* and the *Getty* are really popular. And the *MOCA*. I usually choose a museum based on what the current exhibit is. But LA's the second biggest city in the US, so there are plenty of museums here. There's even a *Los Angeles Police Museum*, believe it or not, although I've never been.

And what is something LA offers that no other city has?

The Los Angeles Police Museum. No, seriously, the Latin culture. There are not many cities in the US where you can feel it like you do here. Hispanics make up 48% of the population compared to 27% white, 15% Asian, and 9% black. Check out Olivera Street, the oldest part of Downtown LA for more traditional Mexican culture. Or the Boyle Heights area on Cesar Chavez has a lot of small shops and restaurants if you want to experience the East LA that Cheech and Chong sang about in the 1980s (although they're originally from Canada).

What do you wish for LA's future?

I'd like to see the Metro used more and made more convenient for the people. The subway system doesn't have so many stations—if you want to go to one, you need to use your car, and once you're in your car, you don't use the Metro.

I really wish they'd create a bullet train to San Francisco. By plane it's a one-hour flight, but it's expensive and a big hassle. By car it's seven hours. The Amtrak train takes 12 hours I believe. If they did a train that went in even two or three hours, many people would use it.

Urban Nexus

The vertical, industrialised answer to LA's suburban sprawl, Downtown's story is one of rebirth. From gritty wasteland to epicentre of cool, the DTLA skyline is as full of history as it is surprises

Culture | **Art on the Edge**

Gehry, Basquiat and Kusama alongside emerging regional artists—DTLA's offering is diverse enough to quench the thirst of most art lovers. *The Broad*, newest neighbour to the LA Philharmonic, exhibits a private collection up there with any great city's modern art museum. Note that entrance is free but tickets should be booked in advance. *MOCA's* three locations, meanwhile, focus on relevant art produced after 1940, with Little Tokyo's *Geffen Contemporary* exhibiting in a former police garage. Blurring the lines between art and commerce is *Museum as Retail Space*, an independent exhibition venue featuring regional artists and a shop stocking handmade wares that are both art and object. And proven classic LACMA illuminates with installations like Chris Burden's "Urban Light" (pictured).

• Downtown, various locations, see Index p.63

East 3rd Street is one of LA's few pedestrian havens. Steps away from the infamous American Hotel you'll find *Poketo*, a stationery and hand-made goods store specialising in colourful, quality wares made by local hands. Neighbouring *Apolis* serves up fair trade menswear and art shows with complimentary coffee to boot. Expect to find the owners manning the till and don't be shy to ask for recommendations. Just next door at *Alchemy Works* everything is for sale—even the sweet vintage car in the middle of the room. Settle down with a coffee and a copy of "The Believer" or peruse the Warby Parker showroom.
• Downtown, various locations, see Index p.63

Shop | Page Filler

Despite what its name would indicate, *The Last Bookstore* in DTLA is a beacon of hope for brick-and-mortar booksellers everywhere. Spanning an impressive 2,000 square metres, the two-storey shop houses a gallery space in collaboration with a local art collective, an adorable little shop that stocks locally-made stationery, and its very own vinyl and graphic novel departments. Upstairs in the rare books section, walk through the tunnel of tomes to reach a sci-fi lover's fantasy—an entire section dedicated to antique editions.
• The Last Bookstore, 453 S Spring St, Downtown, lastbookstorela.com

Food | Mexicano Moderno

Any LA foodie up on their Mexican cuisine will point to *B.S. Taqueria* and *Broken Spanish*. Chef Ray García is the man behind both establishments, whose fresh takes on Mexican staples have brought him a sweeping triumph on the Los Angeles food scene. While B.S. Taquería offers informal treats like churros, tacos and rice and beans in a kitschy, youthful atmosphere, Broken Spanish caters to finer diners with dishes like reimagined tamales and fresh snapper.
• Downtown, various locations, see Index p.63

Italian Duel

The Arts District is growing faster than you can say "craft cocktail", which means the culinary offering is, these days, far from scant. On one end of the spectrum awaits pro skater-owned *Pizzanista* (pictured). Sit at the counter and take in all the Thrasher paraphernalia along the walls while punk rock blasts from the stereo. On Sundays two American obsessions are united in their mac 'n' cheese pizza. For a more proper dining experience, *Bestia*'s friendly staff serves up well-executed Mediterranean cuisine like gnocchi with bone marrow and a home-run plate of mussels and clams. Book ahead.
• Downtown, various locations, see Index p.63

Night | **Sigue la Fiesta**

For those in search of an authentic night out in Tinseltown, look no further than *La Cita*; where tequila, a well-worn dance floor and more than enough neon await. The traditional Latin dance club hosts DJ nights that run the gamut from hip hop and dancehall to house and techno. Come for Mustache Mondays, the club's weekly gay night, to find the most diverse crowd—straight and gay—this side of the border.
• La Cita, 336 S Hill St, Downtown, lacitabar.com

Food | **Condimental Shift**

This Oaxacan classic is LA's go-to restaurant for all matters *mole*. Let the always-present Mexican crooners serenade you from the stage as you take your pick of mole negro, coloradito or amarillo to go over your tamales or empanadas (two musts from the menu). The family-run *Guelaguetza* has been around for over 20 years —it will only take one bite to understand why.
• Guelaguetza, 3014 W Olympic Blvd, Koreatown, ilovemole.com

Food · Night **Blue Hour Living**

From lounging in the sun to star-lit cocktails, everything seems better 20 floors up. LA has been called "72 suburbs in search of a city"—and its rooftops provide a fresh perspective. Fine dining and a breathtaking view await atop a skyscraper at *Perch*, a gilded-age haven with only glass barriers separating diners from the heavens. For those in search of livelier horizons, Koreatown's *The Line Hotel* offers a well-catered pool experience alongside veggie-focussed fare in *Commissary*. The restaurant inside a greenhouse offers clever re-works of Americana classics like spam and eggs and Klondike bars. Tip: Head downstairs to arcade/bar hybrid *Break Room 86* for afterhours entertainment. *Upstairs Bar at The Ace Hotel*, meanwhile, offers something from early morning to early morning thanks to an open pool, a short and sweet menu and a colourful selection of cocktails named after native Californian bird species. Daytime DJ sets presented by local radio Dublab make for an excellent way to relax alongside some of LA's musically-minded. Finally, an astroturf deck, heated pool, waterbeds and a German-style beer garden are on offer chez *The Rooftop at The Standard*, where DJs spin into the summer nights. Head up on weeknights to avoid crowds, and drink in the surrounding sprawl.

• Downtown, various locations, see Index p.63

Shana Mabari, Artist
Individual Growth

As a Los Angeles native who's travelled the world and lived in Paris and Tel Aviv, Shana Mabari values the old-school appeal of Los Angeles. She's always abreast of the latest art shows in the local galleries—and has shared some of her insights with LOST iN

According to somebody born in Los Angeles... Where is the essence of the city to be found?

The essence of Los Angeles is everywhere, there is no centre. Each person finds a purely unique connection with the city individual to themselves, who they are, what they do, and how they shape their vision and direction in life. But if I had to choose one: I grew up in the Fairfax district, so that is my centre. Artist Robbie Conal once referred to *Canter's Deli* on Fairfax Avenue as the centre of Los Angeles, which I have to agree with.

"Illumetric"—your triptych of sculptures—is shown on Santa Monica Boulevard. Where else in the city should one go to see art in the public space and outdoors?

There is incredible public art scattered all around the city. "Illumetric" is part of the City of West Hollywood's "Art on the Outside"—an ongoing public art program that rotates works at locations in the city's parks and on its medians. *LACMA* has great works on the museum grounds open to the public, including Chris Burden's "Urban Light" and Michael Heizer's "Levitated Mass." Jonathan Borofsky's "Molecule Man" at the Federal Building Downtown is a favourite, and Paul Tzanetopoulos's "LAX Pylons" change colour as you fly in and out of the airport. I also sometimes think of architecture as public art. Eric Owen Moss's "Hayden Tract" on Jefferson Boulevard changes light colours periodically. I pass by each day on the way home from my studio so it's exciting to discover what colour will be glowing that evening. At times I consider bridges and freeway ramps similar to public art. The compositions as you drive through the intricate engineered structures are stunning.

Artist Catherine Opie has an incredible series of photographs "Freeways". They really capture the essence of architecture, design and composition in the freeway overpass ramps in Los Angeles.

What are your favourite galleries?

Hauser Wirth & Schimmel's new gallery in the Arts District is worth a visit. Other places I try to visit regularly are *Regen Projects* and *Kohn Gallery* in Hollywood, and *Gagosian Gallery* in Beverly Hills. *Honor Fraser Gallery* and *Edward Cella Gallery* in Culver City have great shows, *William Turner Gallery* at Bergamot Station and *Rosamund Felsen Gallery* Downtown are also favourites. It's also always great to see new emerging talent at *Gallery 825*, the Los Angeles Art Association's exhibit space.

If friends are visiting—where would you take them on a weekend to surprise them?

Sometimes new lovers of the city try to be so original with their findings that they forget to enjoy the extravagance of old school Los Angeles. It's always a pleasure to spend an afternoon at *Barneys New York* in Beverly Hills to peruse the shoe department and lunch at the rooftop restaurant *Freds*. When in Little Tokyo I get my ramen fix at *Orochon* which is always packed. *Tacos Villa Corona* in Atwater Village has the best breakfast burritos—if you can catch them before they close at 1pm. *Zinque* in West Hollywood and *Venice Beach Wines* are wonderful spots for enjoying a drink and snack on the patio.

On the Move

David Labi

From gangs to gentrification, Los Angeles is a city of constant change

For decades, Los Angeles has been named the "gang capital of America". At the city's worst period in the 1990s, 10,000 young people were killed over ten years. That's double the US soldiers killed in a decade of war in Iraq. And the figure doesn't count those who lost limbs, eyesight, peace of mind—and their liberty.

This pool of tragedy has had a glamorous sheen applied to it by gangster rap: seminal 1988 album "Straight Outta Compton" by NWA placed the district south of LA on the map. Rival Compton gangs the Crips and the Bloods—in their warring colours of red and blue—became idolised by teenagers the world over.

Echo Park is up there with Compton as a historic gangland. Its groups are manifold, with cabaret names like Echo Park Locos, Big Top Locos, Crazys, Diamond Street Locos, Frogtown and Head Hunters. Once, they ruled the hood, carrying out drive-by shootings and painting tags on walls in a constant graffiti war to mark territory.

Gangs have a complex relationship with their communities, providing a binding force as well as a destructive one. The Diamond Street Locos, for example, joined forces with local gay activists in the 1970s to stem a tide of homophobic attacks and run an annual community fair that lasted 30 years. Yet, they still found time to murder members of rival gangs and accidentally kill a four-year-old kid with a stray bullet. The net effect is clear.

But things have changed in Echo Park: encapsulating a wider transformation in the city. One US magazine recently cited it the best neighbourhood in the whole country. The fact the publication is called "Money" gives an unsubtle hint to the forces at work. In 2013, the Echo Park lake was dredged. Surprisingly only three guns were found—and no dead bodies. New waters, new beginnings.

But is it premature to proclaim the "end of gangs"? Gang crime reportedly halved over 2008–2014. Streets are clear of intimidating congregations, walls bare of graffiti tags, young black men openly stroll in Latin strongholds like Hawaiian Gardens without fear—after a decade of indiscriminate "brown on black" killings. In Compton, unemployment was slashed from 18% to 11%, there's large-scale investment and a gang truce is in place. Could the curse have been lifted?

Forces at Work

Massive reform in the LAPD—both in approach and strategy—has played a huge part in the sea change. Today's force is a far cry from the hated institution widely blamed for some of the worst civil unrest in US history.

In 1992, an unarmed black motorist was beaten by police officers—and the event was caught on camera. The motorist's name was Rodney King. And when the officers were acquitted of using excessive force, violence exploded across the African-American neighbourhoods of South Central and beyond, for six days.

The cartoon villain was despised police chief Daryl Gates. His militaristic philosophy of brutal suppression had been neatly summed up by the name of one of his campaigns: "Operation Hammer". The LAPD was a law unto itself—with minimum numbers and maximum violence it acted like an occupying army.

Then came the Rampart Scandal in the late 1990s. Widespread corruption was uncovered in a special gangs unit. Offenses included planting evidence, shooting innocents, selling confiscated drugs. One officer even robbed $722,000 from the Bank of America. The LAPD was put under oversight of the US Justice Department in 2001 until it could sort itself out. Community policing became a focus, diversity among officers was increased, chiefs openly criticised the excessive use of force... Approval ratings among minorities shot up.

But the LAPD's softer approach has been a velvet glove masking an iron hand. At the same time cops have worked closely with prosecutors and federal agents to wage a legal war on gangs. The RICO statute against organised crime— originally used against Italian mafia in the 1970s—has meant gang members can be imprisoned wholesale. Hundreds of people have been locked away over the last 15 years.

Meanwhile, the gang injunction has cleared streets. Using it, police can arrest people for even being seen together in public. In Echo Park for example, the above-named local outfits have been prohibited from fraternising in a 3.8-square-mile "safety zone". This has made "corner boys" a thing of the past.

So where are the gangs? Prisons are full to bursting, for a start. The US has one inmate for every 108 citizens—barring North Korea (perhaps), the highest in the world. But this is merely a temporary displacement of society's ills. "The prison system is not to safeguard communities," says LA expert Mike Davis, "but to warehouse hatred for the day when it returns to the street." Prisons themselves are ruled by gangs, and released members have new allegiances and old scores to settle.

But many gangs have simply moved away—due to the more prosaic reason of gentrification. "Money" magazine's darling Echo Park lost a piece of its identity in mid-2015 when El Batey Number 2 Market closed doors. New owners converted the building into "The Grafton Lofts" and asked for $6,000 a month. Market-owner Evelia Diaz had been a feature of the block for half a century.

Parallel is the gang disappearance. In Echo Park, the "EXP" of Echo Park Locos and the "CZY" of the Crazys now only appear on Mondays, after gangsters have travelled in from spots like Inland Empire and El Sereno to hang out. Officers call them a "weekend gang". When a Locos leader was shot by his own gang in 2009, the shooter had driven in from Pasadena. A commuter shooter.

Mass RICO jailings keep gangsters out the way for a couple of years. They come back to find no friends around and rents they can't touch. Newbies have little clue about the hood's complex history— they don't know their neighbours. Gentrification has transformed Echo Park's colour profile, with the white population almost doubling over ten years.

Compton might well follow suit. The city was once a white middle-class haven—before a huge postwar influx of African-Americans. The 1965 Watts Riots stimulated the "white flight" from South Central, and Compton hit a high of 73% black. Now it's 70% Latino. But house prices are rising—the first Compton house was recently posted at $1 million. With the "Hub City"'s strategic location and corporate makeover, the gentrifying army is not far away. And they're usually white.

Racial Roots

Though Los Angeles constantly reinvents itself, the past remains in the texture of today. Gangs and gentrification might seem new phenomena. But the same processes have been going on since the city's birth.

In 1779 Spanish colonists kicked out Tongva Indians to establish their settlement. The town eventually became a Mexican city, and was later inducted into the States. When Anglo cattle ranchers flooded in around the 1880s, they weren't satisfied with the old city centre, the Plaza. So they built their own, a mile away—Pershing Square. Instead of integrating into the existing city, the whites effectively re-founded it.

That's what passed for town planning in Los Angeles, and has been much the way ever since. Enforced segregation has been replaced with market forces that achieve a similar result.

In the 1880s, LA's Chinese community used the market to stake their claim in the city. When new taxes targeted the growing community, they took action. Chinese vendors sold most of the city's vegetables, so they went on strike. A few days without greens and officials were forced to renegotiate. The community was still scarred by the Chinese massacre

of 1871, in which 18 people were tortured and lynched after a white rancher was caught in the crossfire of a Chinatown dispute. The Chinese Angelenos remained despite efforts to scare them off. When their buildings were burned down in a wave of arson attacks in the late 1880s, they simply started rebuilding a few blocks away.

But their downtown location was attractive to planners of a 20th-century metropolis. Hence in the 1920s it was chosen as the site for a new rail terminus: Union Station. This decision was, according to historian Mark Wild, "racialised corporate urban development". Chinatown, though functional for the goods and services it provided, was deemed unsavoury to have in plain sight.

LA residents voted to build Union Station on the historic Mexican central square. But efforts by conservationists led to its preservation as a romanticised memorial to the city's Spanish-American past. It's now a prime tourist destination, which typifies how marginalised communities are today commodified to give unique "character" to a city. Chinatown—which draws tourists, creates business and contributes to LA's multicultural credentials—was only built in its present location after the original one had a station dropped on it.

Another LA landmark—Dodgers Stadium—also obliterated a community. The valley of Chavez Ravine was an idyll where generations of Mexican-Americans had lived almost self-sufficiently. In 1949 the city received federal money to build public houses. They kicked out residents, giving little or no compensation. And the public houses weren't built. Among cries of "Communism!" property developers opposed the bill, a government official was jailed, and the land rebought at a painfully knock-down price. Only to be sold to the Dodgers, who moved from Brooklyn to shore up LA's sporting landscape. Another tile in the city's modern mosaic.

The Latino community of Chavez Ravine had little recourse to rights to protest their removal from the zone, despite the so-called end of segregation. LA had started out with enforced division: certain races and ethnicities couldn't live in certain areas. Beaches and schools were segregated. When this was ruled unconstitutional it was replaced by workarounds. One was the restrictive covenant—a clause in homeowners' contracts that they couldn't sell to non-whites. Another was redlining, when financial institutions would refuse to give loans to minorities buying in certain areas.

Today these legal restrictions are gone. But LA remains segregated. According to the "Racial Dot Map" from the University of Virginia, it's number one for white-Hispanic segregation in the US. Says expert Camilla Z. Charles, "What is problematic about segregation is primarily about the concentration of poverty". Hence the flipside—an area's increase in wealth causes communities to concentrate elsewhere.

A bizarre side effect of these forces was it wasn't white middle class people who bore the brunt of the 1992 Rodney King riots. It was Koreans. A Korean shopkeeper had recently shot dead a black teenager, which ignited an oil tanker of resentment. Koreans had established Koreatown in the 1970s. Mostly highly educated back home, stiff competition pushed them to the States, where they invested in deprived areas opening groceries and liquor stores. Poverty raised tension and African-Americans and Koreans suffered a clash of cultural misunderstanding fuelled by media sensationalism. When the riots broke out, black gang members looted about 2,000 Korean businesses, burning many to the ground. Many Koreans fought back, shooting from their rooftops. This was prime viewing at the birth of the 24-hour news culture. The riots were contained by police: they didn't intervene, instead setting up a perimeter. The perception was they were letting the communities fight it out, so long as it didn't bleed into any white neighbourhoods. After six days the army moved in to put a stop to it—but the damage was done.

Heavy-handed processes are no longer required to change a zone's racial make-up. Much maligned hipsterism as a vanguard of gentrification does the job. But plenty of middle-class whites are also priced out of burgeoning zones, too. Echo Park houses are beyond the reach of many and are only going in one direction—as privileged sections of LA get even richer.

Santa Monica is currently LA's most expensive neighbourhood, with the average dwelling going for a snip at $3.1 million. To think even this area was once ruled by gangs. Remnants of Santa Monica 13 still hang on in one of the last enclaves of Westside gangbanging. Some 15 years ago soul searching ensued when a Chicano-themed mural at nearby Stoner Park was taken down for restoration of a building. The mural represented cooperation between the Sotel gang and locals. "Restoration" tends to blot out features of the past, while imposing new problems for the future.

David Labi is a London-born writer, editor and filmmaker who has travelled the world finding stories and losing himself. He's currently based in Berlin

Nana Ghana
She is a creative presence who
glitters across the artistic fields.
As model she was chosen to
represent Stella McCartney's line
in LA. As actress she recently
worked on the Nina Simone
biopic "Nina". And as filmmaker,
her feature documentary "LA
Woman Rising", narrated by
James Franco, is putting a new
spin on female identity in the city

Nana Ghana, Filmmaker & Actress

Rising Woman

LA is a city of creativity, history and spirituality—all themes explored
by Nana Ghana in her chat with LOST iN. The multi-talented artist
mused on the quintessential LA woman, recommended vintage shopping and edgy art, and salivated over the world's best taco—as well
as naming some spots for outdoor inspiration

How did you end up in LA?

I was born in Ghana, but I came to LA to be in film. I was modelling in NYC at the time, but coming to LA was something I felt very strongly about. Before I moved here I went to a film academy and it was the first time discovering California. The palm trees, the vast skies, the weather, the ocean and the mountains... So I finished my plan and I was like, "I'm going to LA."

Your recent film "LA Woman Rising" documented 50 women's morning routines. What did it tell you about the female Angeleno?

When I began that project it was actually to illuminate what the real LA woman was like. I felt like the LA woman was often misconstrued. Even one of the women in the film says the LA woman is blond with fake boobs and doesn't have a job. So I think I've humanised who the LA woman is. She's many things: a Latina from Southgate, a Beverly Hills woman, the taco truck lady, the transwoman in West Hollywood, a mother, a grandmother... She wants to work hard, that's part of who she is. The film's title says "rising". It's about their pursuit of their dreams, not adhering to their impediment, or what neighbour-hood they belong to.

Speaking of neighbourhoods, which one do you belong to?

Koreatown, for two years now. I was in Venice Beach for so fucking long, it became so gentrified. For me as an artist, it was important to be in a place I can afford, where there's life, there's something hap-pening. I'm loving Koreatown, I love the Korean culture and interactions with the people here, the clash of the Mexican culture. Also being anonymous... I can go and get a coffee quickly, go to the gym, the spa, because it's literally in the middle of the city—it's the perfect location for me. And the history is so wonderful. During the Roaring Twenties it was where the actors and music stars lived. I love feeling like I'm living in a building that has culture and history because LA is such a new city, everything's so modern—you don't normally have that connection.

Where do you go for high fashion with a twist?

My friends have a shop in Venice called *Principessa*, it's such a lovely shop. *Stella McCartney* is great, I love how conscious her line is. But I buy a lot of vintage. At the *Santee Alley* downtown in the Fashion District, they sell all these cute little things for a dollar, five dollars. I go to a party and people are like "Oh my god, where did you get that?" Actually I shouldn't be telling you this, the secret will come out.

Where are your favourite outdoor places to go for inspiration?

I love the ocean. *Malibu Beach*. I love driving up the coast, and driving and finding a secluded area on the beach to relax, or catch up with friends. I love the *Griffith Observatory* in Hollywood. I love the *Huntington Gardens*. And *The Getty* of course, oh my god I forgot about that! It's so beautiful. The endless garden... You can have a picnic, roll in the gardens, read and drink some wine.

And what about finding on-the-cusp art that gets the juices flowing?

I find a lot of things that I'm inspired by online. DTLA is the pulse for the arts scene for sure, but for me, I like discovering new artists and that kind of vibe for sure, like my girlfriend is doing a piece right now at the *Chainlink Gallery*. It's run by this girl Cheryl

Asian-inspired club Blind Dragon hosts blistering DJ nights under a carpark

Commissary at the
Line Hotel
Koreatown

Chateau Marmont
West Hollywood

Blind Dragon
West Hollywood

who came to LA and started this gallery and is showing women, giving people a chance. Personally I try to live between both worlds, I go out to seek inspiration, but I also go within.

How should outsiders approach the city?

Have a very open mind, an open heart. LA's not like any other city, it's so spread out, there's so many neighbourhoods. You can live in Beverly Hills and not have anything to do with DTLA. So when a person comes to LA they have to remain curious and open and know that it takes a year to discover. I'm still discovering after ten years.

If you had a friend coming to stay with you, how would you spend the day... and the night?

I'd Uber to the airport to pick

them up. Then we'd come home, I'd take them to the *Line Hotel* in Koreatown for lunch, maybe go to a spa and do some relaxation. Then we'd drive up to *Griffith Park* to watch the sunset. We'd come back home and take a disco nap. From there, *Chateau Marmont* for dinner, because it's really close. I love the steak frites all day. All day! Then we'd call up our friend and go up the hill to the house. I'm not really into bars. We'd put up the music, massage the music. Then we'd hit up *Blind Dragon*, this new club, it's so great. There's an amazing LA DJ there, still under-cover but getting an international reputation: Miles Hendricks. He DJs there and it's so wild. It's underneath this parking lot and it's all Asian-themed. We'd go and have a kiki and then Uber home.

What about if you had to plan the perfect romantic date?

We'd go to the Chateau, get a room all day, then eat all night (laughs). *The Ace Hotel* is also a really special place to stay. There's a romantic place for dinner, *Hama Sushi* in Little Tokyo—it's so good, it's traditional Japanese. It's very small so you have to wait an hour, but it's so worth it.

You're a frequent collaborator with James Franco. Do you have a traditional haunt to bat ideas around?

We usually go to Chateau, grab a bungalow there.

How about to see movies? An authentic LA movie palace?

The movie theatre on Fairfax, the *Silent Movie Theatre* is really cool. I recently went to the *Sundance Cinemas*, it was also pretty cool.

And what do you do to relax?

I meditate all the time. On my altar I have different candles, different colours depending on what I want to reach. I have my herbs, my smudges that I use, my incenses and my oils, my clear water. Meditation is something we all have to do. I never really thought about myself as an artist until I moved to LA, I think people forget what the real purpose of the art is. In the modern world, the most important thing has been cut out. Getting together and having conversations with people—that's the key to creativity and having a better life, I think.

Where's good to go in Koreatown?

All the Korean barbeque is the shit... Just go to any place on 6th Street. For drinks, the *Café Brass Monkey* right here is pretty cool. Then there's *The Prince*, it's super art deco but super weird, it looks like a David Lynch movie. Oh I forgot the *Slurpin' Ramen Bar* is also round here in Koreatown, it's a great new ramen place. And one more bar worth going to is Keith Sutherland's *R Bar*.

And finally... where are the best tacos?

Venice on Rose and 4th, that taco truck. I binge on it. The carnitas tacos, and it has the best chicken quesadilla. It's a regional taco—the way they marinate the carnitas, they're so crispy. Mmm, maybe I'm going to go to Venice today...

"A backyard BBQ celebrating the farms and the streets" is encased in the greenhouse of Commissary at the Line Hotel

Vivid Clarity

A photo showcase by George Byrne

Capturing that particular way the sun hits Los Angeles, George Byrne's photographs spin LA's disposable architecture and redundant landscapes into neat geometry, thoughtful shadows and poetic stillness. From 2013, his Instagram @george_byrne has become a popular extension of his art practice. Following, a selection from Byrne's 2016 exhibition "Local Divisions"

Stella Blu & Anwar Taj Washington, Artist & Fashion Designer

Cultural Fabric

**Stella Blu &
Anwar Taj Washington**
She is an artist who uses water-colours and graphite to create paintings of surreal fantasies. Originally from Sri Lanka, she draws her inspiration from deities. He is a streetwear designer, who founded his first line in 2007 and later broke off to launch "Carrots by Anwar". The couple's careers and inspiration often overlap, with Anwar incorporating Stella's creations onto clothing designs while she reproduces portraits of him

Living and working in Mid-Wilshire, Anwar and Stella are part of LA's generation of young creators. Here, the couple offer us a glimpse into the expansive world of their city's art and streetwear scene, complete with the best tacos and favourite outdoor hangout spots

You've both lived in a lot of different parts of the world—why did you settle in LA?

Anwar: I chose to settle in Los Angeles after discovering my love for contemporary street fashion. I happened to move here while it was at its forefront culturally. The difference between LA and other cities in my opinion would have to be the opportunity. Anything you want to achieve or become in any field of work is right here in this city. Anything you even thought of trying to accomplish, this is a great place to try it out. No rules—go get it and succeed!

Stella: I originally came to LA just for city experience since I had grown up a little sheltered with my parents. Then I stuck around for a few more years and settled here after I started dating Anwar. There's a lot to do in this city, a lot of different foods to try, and different events to go to. That's why it's different from so many other cities. You can have bomb Korean food in Koreatown one night and then the next you're grabbing bomb Ethiopian food in Little Ethiopia. It's been fun exploring all the things LA has to offer. I've got to try a lot of things I've never tried before.

What part of LA do you live in now? What are some of the highlights there?

Stella: We live in the Mid-Wilshire area. The best part is we're really centrally located around so many other cool districts and neighbourhoods. We have access to so many different types of foods and places... Little Ethiopia, Little Tokyo, Koreatown, *Grand Central Market*, *The Farmers' Market at the Grove*. They are all cool places to check out if you've never been before.

What were your favourite spots growing up here?

Anwar: I was born in Trenton, New Jersey, but was raised in Orlando, Florida. I was also raised in St. Thomas US Virgin Islands and LA. Growing up in LA my favourite spots as a teen were The Grove, Pan Pacific Park, and The Beverly Center. Those were my kick-it spots with my friends. Great area to grow up around.

Stella: Actually Anwar's lived in LA longer than I have, I moved to LA after high school. My favourite spots were always by the beach. I loved hanging out in Venice, Abbot Kinney, Santa Monica. There's a lot of shops, restaurants, bars, cool people, and fun things going on in those areas. Especially on the weekends.

Stella, can you suggest your favourite galleries in town?

Stella: If you've been following the influence and taste of Moran Bondaroff from his days with Supreme up to now, you should go see what he curates at his gallery *Moran Bondaroff*. Also, as one of the newborns of contemporary art galleries, *Mama Gallery* is becoming one of LA's Art District go-to galleries. For the lovers of pop art, art from the modern masters, and whimsical pieces you should check out the *Kohn Gallery*. I miss the little spot he had on Beverly Boulevard that Retna painted. As an artist, to be represented by *The Gagosian* would be ideal! From their exhibits to the gift shop everything is done with precision and great taste. There are over 15 Gagosians in the world. So if you get a chance to visit this contemporary art gallery I suggest you check it out. From the landscaping to the art, the *Getty Center* is one of my favourite museums. You get a great view of the city from the Getty as well! Everyone should take time to check out Eli Broad's extensive collection at *The Broad*—it's free but you have to reserve tickets in advance. If you get there at an early time, make sure you check out Yayoi Kusama's "Infinity Mirrored Room".

Anwar, are there any fashion stores or LA brands that stand out to you?
    Anwar: *Babylon* is one of my favourite shops, aesthetically speaking, in Los Angeles. It's owned by the Trash Talk punk band signed to Odd Future Records. If you love zines, skate, and punk culture this shop is for you. I love the burning palm tree logo. *424 on Fairfax* is the perfect shop that bridges the gap between contemporary street fashion and high-end fashion. Golf Wang is my favourite brand out of Los Angeles by a great figure in pop culture and also a great friend of mine, Tyler, the Creator. He's creating pieces with beneath-the-surface messages displayed through his graphics, exuberant colours, and great aesthetic. Hey, if you're a golf fan as well I'm sure you'll love it. When it comes to young men bettering themselves and becoming businessmen, great skate, quirky and fun illustration on garments, art shows, and just flat out fun, *Illegal Civilization*. Then there's *Passport Harun Collective*. Walking into PHC you get a whiff of essential body oils that are exclusive to the shop. Books on African culture, shoes made in Africa, garments with African influence and a splash of hip hop influence, all there on Beverly Boulevard. While shopping you may run into one of your favourite rappers. From Rodarte to their eclectic shop tees designed by artist Alexis Ross, I love the *Virgil Normal shop*—not only for the brands they carry but also the location. It's one of those shops that creates this vibe of comfort while shopping. They also have

a great back patio for events and pop-ups. *Born x Raised* is a brand I love for the simple fact that it has stayed true to its name. They were born and raised in Venice California, pulling inspiration from their own culture, from gang banging to Native American history. Amazing placements as far as graphics—and their font is amazing!

And what are the best spots to find street art here?
    Stella: The best area for street art would have to be the Art District, Downtown Los Angeles. Also there's the Downtown LA Art Walk to check some cool art, I think it's every second Thursday of the month.

What is the most romantic spot in the city?
    Stella: I find driving to Malibu down the Pacific Coast Highway really romantic. You can stop and eat—there's a few cute spots to stop and have a romantic meal or grab dessert and a coffee, then catch the sunset on the beach. Definitely my type of romance. Malibu Country Mart is a nice outdoor shopping area to walk around. *Escondido Falls* is a little hike with beautiful waterfalls if you're more active.
    Anwar: I couldn't agree more with you.

Where do you go for a night-cap?
    Stella: *El Carmen* on 3rd Street is a good place for cocktails, tequila, also delicious quick snacks.
    Anwar: Yes, *Sake House Miro*'s sunomuno (cucumber salad) and hot sake is amazing!

Since there aren't really seasons in LA, what are your favourite year-round outdoor spots?
    Stella: We love to go hiking. *Culver City* stairs is a good

Housed in a labyrinthine warehouse, Mama Gallery is boldly shaking up the Arts District

workout, *Topanga State Park* is a great hike with some really nice scenery. We also love to catch the farmers' markets, there's many around Los Angeles. On Sundays, *Studio City Farmers' Market* has some really yummy produce and foods.

Who makes the best taco in town?
  Anwar: I'd say the *El Chato* taco truck on La Brea and Olympic.
  Stella: I would say *El Carmen* on 3rd street because I mostly eat a vegetarian diet and sometimes fish. El Carmen has delicious fish tacos, and a good potato one. For vegans, *Café Gratitude* in Larchmont! LA has good tacos for everyone.

East of Eden

Thrilling times in northeast LA, where new populations are blending with history to create a diverse cocktail of cuisine and culture. Echo Park and Silver Lake are further along in the process, while Highland Park and Eagle Rock are on the sweet cusp of change right now

Culture | **Deep House**

The *Neutra-VDL* building was home and studio to architect Richard Neutra, and one of his first buildings in the US after he moved over from Austria in the 1920s. Arguably the origin of hi-tech, indoor-outdoor Californian modernism, it now belongs to Cal Poly Pomona College of Environmental Design. Take the tour given by Cal Poly students Saturdays 11am-3pm and marvel at how the light falls through the windows. Further treasures can be gawped at on a circuit of Silver Lake. East side of the water on Windsor Avenue, stand two early-1970s wood-panelled houses. These were designed by Barton Choy to reflect a "sea ranch aesthetic". And north on Micheltorena Street sits a concrete-topped UFO with panelled glass walls, looking like it inspired one of the LA cults. This is the 1963 Reiner-Burchill Residence—architect John Lautner's first foray into the monolithic use of concrete.
• Neutra VDL Studio and Residences, 2300 Silver Lake Blvd, Silver Lake, neutra-vdl.org

Breakthrough Brunch

The unlikely blend of French and Mexican fare at *Trois Familia* might leave you forever craving bechamel sauce on your nachos. Set in a Silver Lake strip mall, the café is available only for brunch, for which you'll be seated next to strangers at one of six communal tables. Friendly, well-coiffed servers bring hybrid gems like chorizo galettes, French onion quesadillas and grits with mole butter and creme fraiche. The owners have two other restaurants in LA, all sprung from their joy in adventurous dishes.
• Trois Familia, 3510 Sunset Boulevard, Silver Lake, troisfamilia.com

Shop **Uncommon Wealth**

Hemingway and Pickett is what gift shops want to be when they grow up. Aussie owner Toby Burke Hemingway keeps a well-curated showroom of jewelry, ceramics, art prints and artfully-designed home wares, most of them handmade in Australia or California. The building was last occupied by the store and event space *Otherwild*, which has relocated to Los Feliz where it continues to celebrate local artists and designers of intersectional feminist swag.
• Hemingway and Pickett, 1932 Echo Park Ave, hemingwayandpickett.com

Food **Hands-on Dining**

A bright Thai joint that's just so LA—*Night + Market Song's* neon walls are decorated with holographic Michael Jackson and topless Cindy Crawford posters. The menu strays from the traditional, with crowd favourites like the fried chicken and papaya slaw sandwich. Use your hands to eat the sticky rice and infamous spicy larb—advice that comes from the chef's authentic roots. Kris Yenbamroong is heavy-handed with the roast chillies and spices, which he apparently lugs back from the Thai-Burma border. Be prepared to wait for a table.
• Night + Market Song, 3322 Sunset Blvd, Silver Lake, nightmarketla.com

Mexican Four Ways

Highland Park is rife with kick-ass taco trucks, but the hood also has brick and mortar standbys, each specialising in something different. Find a spot inside *Metro Balderas* for Mexico City-style gorditas—small, stuffed cakes—that taste like fat little miracles. For carne asada fries with kick and Southern sopes, head to *My Taco*. And if you're curious for less familiar Mexican food, *El Faisán y El Venado* does home-style Yucatán—try the panuchos, or topped, fried tortillas. And for huaraches—heavenly loaded squares of dough—*El Huarache Azteca* is your joint. Eating here is like pulling up a chair at the family dinner table.
• Highland Park, various locations, see Index p.63

Food **Pig Out**

Entrepreneurial LA chef Andre Guerrero is pioneering what he calls "slow fast food" on Colorado Boulevard, the hip thoroughfare of flourishing Eagle Rock. *The Oinkster* has a $10-and-under menu that nevertheless refuses to skimp on quality. Slow-roasted pork, house-cured pastrami, and Gruyère alongside the signature Aberdeen Angus burgers with extra crispy Belgian-style fries and home-made ketchups. With all those specialist ingredients you'll be sure to find long queues of burger-hungry bearded folk.
• The Oinkster, 2005 Colorado Boulevard, Eagle Rock, theoinkster.com

Night **To the Cave**

When former gothic dive bar Little Cave changed its name to *La Cuevita*, the Mexican theme arrived in force. The bikers and gangsters of Highland Park's past were replaced by a wide selection of tequilas and mezcals, including the famous Del Maguey line—from the lower end to the handcrafted Pechuga. A daily happy hour from 7-10pm makes it quite feasible to try various of their cocktail creations, including the Mezcalada featuring roasted poblano peppers. A taquero comes onsite Tuesdays to whip up that quintessential snack.
• La Cuevita, 5922 N Figueroa Street, Highland Park, lacuevitabar.com

Shop | Second Chance

If LA's blood runs thick with vintage clothing and antique decór stores, then Eagle Rock is the heart. Its key arteries are Eagle Rock, Colorado and York Boulevards—but follow your intuition into side streets in search of gold. *Snivling Sibbling* is a neighbourhood favourite for 1920–30s and mid-century décor. On the same style tip is *Sunbeam Vintage*, covering more ground with its enviable selection of mid-century and modern artworks and design pieces. Analogue tappers should head to *US Office Machine Co* for immaculate vintage typewriters. It's run by charming serviceman Ruben, who started out helping his dad in the shop when he was ten. The same street features *The Bearded Beagle*, with a selection of unique US vintage clothing, as well as core items like Levi's 501s at the neighbourhood's fairest prices. Rolling down York, you'll be hard pressed to go home empty handed. *Urchin* is loaded with 1950-70s garb, while *Honeywood* (pictured) is a dream wardrobe for the bohemian wanderer. The opening hours of *The Stash on York* are irregular, or by appointment, but it's worth the trouble. Meanwhile *Weepah Way* is more refined than your typical vintage store: alongside an extensive denim collection, they have beautiful ceramics, jewellery and woven bags. And for vintage food —yes, this is a thing—*Galco's Old World Grocery* will provide nostalgic snacks, sodas and beers.

• Eagle Rock & Highland Park, various locations, see Index p.63

Leah Forester & Bill Johnson
She began her career in styling two decades ago under the mentorship of Diane von Furstenberg and Vera Wang. Since then, the self-professed California girl has made a living working for artists, brands, publications and celebrities. He is a film producer and industry veteran with an expansive filmography under his belt. His company Lotus Entertainment finances, produces and markets big-budget feature films

Leah Forester & Bill Johnson, Stylist & Producer

Familiar Shores

Bill Johnson and Leah Forester discovered they were next-door neighbours after being set up on a date by a friend years ago. These days, the couple still lives in their beloved Venice with their two children, Jett and Jade. From hiking to classical music, they give us a snapshot of LA family life

What does Los Angeles mean to you?

Leah: LA is a city where you can be anything you want to be; life can be lived without rules. It really is a city of dreamers and doers. Here, there are the art, food, and entertainment worlds in full bloom. From Echo Park all the way to the beach are interesting individuals pursuing their dreams and living colourful lives. It's a wonderful city for family life, too, because it has year-round sun, lots of nature if you look for it, and all kinds of school choices.

You still live in the same area you lived in when you met. Why Venice?

Bill: I grew up in Los Angeles and living in Venice is different than anywhere else; you have a sense of urban community that doesn't exist in Hollywood or Hancock Park or Santa Monica. We both love that. Our ocean view is spectacular and we like having a sense of roots for our children. This is the only house they have known, which is different from the gypsy lives we have both led. We just love the heart and soul of Venice. There's an artistic street quality that's real. It still has rough edges and you experience real life, not artificial perfection—the beautiful and the unfortunate.

It's time to grab the kids and go somewhere for quality family time—what's the destination?

Leah: Downtown LA for a day of art, food, and new scenery. Or a quick weekend glamping trip up to *El Capitan Canyon* near Santa Barbara.

Bill, you've worked in the film industry for some time. What should a traveling movie buff check out in LA to avoid classic tourist traps?

Bill: Lunch outside at *The Polo Lounge* in Beverly Hills Hotel, a drive up the Pacific Coast Highway with sunset dinner at *Nobu* Malibu, a night at the *Chateau Marmont*, and a morning hike up *Runyon Canyon*—for a bird's eye view of the city and its people.

Your home is filled with beautiful things—where do you go to buy a present for each other? And for the little ones?

Bill: For each other, we like to make things. Paintings, photo collages, experiences. Otherwise, we take time together during the day and go for lunch and shopping spree, usually at Chanel!

Leah: It's the time we take for each other that's the real gift. For the children, we love *The Acorn Store*, a beautiful natural toy and art supply store in Santa Monica for games, beautiful dolls, or hand-dyed yarn for knitting. On Abbott Kinney we also love *Burro*, which sells cool kids' clothes and books.

Any recommendations for a cheap culinary thrill?

Leah: *Pono Burger*, an organic grass-fed burger joint with delicious sweet potato fries, inside an old steel structure in Santa Monica. They serve classic "fast food" made with quality ingredients. Organic milkshakes for the kids are always a hit.

In Venice it might be easy to forget there's a giant metropolis next door. Are there any places in the city you enjoy visiting as a family?

Bill: We love *Griffith Observatory* in Hollywood for an afternoon of hiking and learning about the cosmos. Another great activity is going to the *Jim Morrison Cave* in Malibu, located high up on a beautiful hike. We usually make a day of breakfast at *Malibu Farm on the Pier*, drive up the Pacific

Above: The vintage-inspired clothing pieces at Christy Dawn are all handmade to last by local artisans
Below: General Store began in San Francisco before spreading its curated and eclectic collection to LA

In a town soaked with sci-fi and Scientology, view the real thing from the Griffith Observatory

Coast Highway, stop at the ocean view kids park on PCH, then continue up to the cave for hiking, exploring and art. You can bring paints and draw on the cave walls with kids—Jim Morrison's drawings are still there.

Leah, your project, Venice Supper Club, is an immersive experience that caters to all the senses—where do you guys go to be pampered?
Leah: A weekend away together is the best way to feel pampered. Just waking up without the daily parental duties and having a long breakfast reading the paper is what we crave. We like to book a room at the Malibu Inn and stay there after a romantic dinner at *Nobu Malibu*. In the morning we go for a long beach walk, read, talk and dream together. Alternately we do adventurous things together like going to Peru or Burning Man—but that's not very relaxing!

It's date night: what's the plan?
Bill: *Soho House* is perfect for a fun, romantic dinner. Meeting at the bar after a long day apart is a great way to reconnect and feel like we are on a date together. There we can eat in the garden and maybe see some live music, all in one place.

Are there any transformations Los Angeles been going through that you're excited about?
Leah: The Downtown LA scene is exciting. After living in New York for many years, I miss the feeling of the urban jungle and in DTLA you still have that feeling.
Bill: It's really all happening down there.The influx of the art world and incredible institutions like *The Broad Museum*, *MOCA* and the *LA Philharmonic* offer so much culture—and that's just on one block!

Bill, where do you go to talk shop?
Bill: The Soho House has the

The poolside Cabana Café at Beverly Hills Hotel gives the hotel's Polo Lounge a run for its money

best view in town. *Hinoki & The Bird* is a cool spot hidden away in Century City and centrally located to all the entertainment agencies. For a relaxed lunch out of the office I often head over to the *Creative Artists Agency* courtyard, which has great architecture and *Craft* restaurant for more formal dining.

LA is full of creative people. Where do you like to pick up beautiful local design?

Leah: Venice is so rich with talent right now. Lincoln Boulevard is becoming the new Abbott Kinney. I love *General Store* for gifts and home accents. *Christy Dawn* is a new shop for romantic gypsy dresses. And *Nick Fouquet* has a little cottage there where he custom makes his incredible hats.

Whether it's for friends abroad or entertaining at home, where do you go when you need to pick up some LA delicacies?

Moon Juice for superfood nutrition gifts like exotic tonics or sage incense. GTA, *Gjelina Take Away,* for last-minute dinner party solutions; the most delicious prepared food! *Gjusta*—Another place by Travis Lett of Gjelina. They sell flowers to go, delicious cakes and other culinary gifts for a hostess. *Café Gratitude* for spiritual gift items like books, journals, and their signature "What are you grateful for?" plates, a lovely gift and souvenir that is classic Venice.

Last, but not least: who makes the best tacos in town?

We do! I'm half Mexican and we have a Taco Tuesday tradition at our house complete with rice, black beans, super fresh organic cilantro, queso fresco and pico de gallo. Everyone custom designs their own version at the Taco Bar in the kitchen.

Venice & Santa Monica
Breezy Vibes

Postcard beaches and exclusive boutiques await in Santa Monica, LA's most expensive area. Venice, a short stroll upcoast, will reveal a colourful contrast thanks to the hippie culture that made it famous

Night	Light my Fire

Santa Monica has a network of plush bars that begs for an upscale cocktail crawl. Below The Victorian, an 1892 stately home, and accessible through a carpark, *The Basement Tavern* is fetchingly kitted out in a former wine cellar, and hosts live rock and reggae almost every night. An extensive bourbon selection can be evaluated in plush leather armchairs. Come early for a quiet drink or late for a more raucous experience. Meanwhile, *Guest Room* can be reached in true speakeasy fashion through a secret entrance in an alley next to Estate restaurant. Touches of leather and dim lighting create an atmosphere perfect for whispering sweet nothings or swapping top secret documents. Creative twists are added to classic cocktails with cordials, chartreuse and an array of bitters. Designed as a rustic cottage with a relaxed vibe, *The Bungalow* feels more like a friend's beach house than a lounge. A very well-appointed friend. The posh seaside shack is complete with charming interiors, fire pits and an outdoor terrace that beckons to come enjoy those famous LA sunsets.

• Various locations, see Index p.63

Hidden Backyard

Famous Venice's Abbot Kinney Boulevard offers a few treasures that could be overlooked. Walk behind a home store with a striking yellow triangle to find the Rabbit Hole, an enclave of specialty shops and eateries. *Another Kind of Sunrise* is a café noteworthy for its signature brew: coffee infused with one spoonful of coconut oil and one of grass-fed butter. Next comes *ZenBunni*, a chocolate shop housed in a refurbished closet —the "rabbit hole" that gives the alley its name. The deal is fair-trade, handmade chocolates made out of raw ingredients.
• The Rabbit Hole, 1629 Abbot Kinney Blvd, Venice, zenbunnichocolate.com

Shop **Blooming Fun**

Combined in one carefully curated boutique are three of life's pleasures: coffee, flowers, and shopping. At *Flowerboy*, pressed flowers line one wall, LA's ubiquitous sunlight streams in through the window and flower petals top the featured drinks and dishes. Visitors can enjoy specialty-brewed coffee paired with pastries or homemade toasts slathered in marmalade or creamy tahini. The boutique offers an eclectic selection of trinkets and furnishings handcrafted by local artists. If you covet anything you see, just ask— everything is up for grabs at Flowerboy.
• Flowerboy, 824 Lincoln Blvd, Venice, flowerboyproject.com

Food **Push the Boat Out**

Swanky Bond villains heading out for seafood in California shouldn't avoid the *Santa Monica Yacht Club*. Despite its name it is not on the beach— but its marine credentials can't be faulted. Here, the East Coast tradition of seafood cuisine meets Californian inspiration, courtesy of chef Andrew Kirschner. Not to be missed is their roasted turbot, which looks like a Jan Švankmajer representation of a fish, and their bass ceviche, doused in coconut water and served in the half shell. The decor fits nicely with an evening cocktail—try the passion fruit pisco sour.
• Santa Monica Yacht Club, 620 Santa Monica Blvd, Santa Monica, eatsmyc.com

Meal Mapping

Joshua Lurie
He's a native of New Jersey who cut his teeth on the East Coast food scene, but has lived as many years in LA. He's a long-time food writer for "LA Weekly", and launched his site "FoodGPS" to help Angelenos navigate their way to the best flavours

The concept of Los Angeles as a melting pot holds particularly true for its restaurant scene. LA is said to provide better sushi than Japan—and the same goes for other national cuisines. The city manages to adopt them, flip them upside down, and make them her own. Joshua Lurie steers us through the city's diverse food offering

El Mar Azul
Highland Park

Guerrilla Tacos
Culver City

Free Range
Various locations

Cassia
Santa Monica

Jun Won
Koreatown

**Elena's Greek-
Armenian Cuisine**
Glendale

Soban
Koreatown

Hatchet Hall
Culver City

N/naka
Culver City

Urasawa
Beverly Hills

CUT
Beverly Hills

Nozawa Bar
Beverly Hills

Q
Downtown

**Beachwood BBQ
& Brewing**
Long Beach

**Matt Biancaniello
pop-up**
Various locations

The Tasting Kitchen
Venice

How did you move from a New Jersey Sopranos diet to LA cuisine?

I grew up about a half-hour from the Sopranos, eating pizza, spaghetti and meatballs, Italian subs... But I've lived in LA just as long as in New Jersey. If it was up to me, I'd have been born in LA, but my parents had other ideas. The experiences kids are exposed to here is staggering. I didn't use chopsticks until I was 21!

What is the state of the LA restaurant nation?

It's interesting you use the term "restaurant nation." LA has a culinary range that can rival some countries. When I have a free meal, I gravitate to family-run spots serving Asian and Middle-Eastern cuisines. LA demonstrates that comfort food knows no bounds.

Getting to the nitty gritty: what are your recommendations for street food?

Though street food is being taken indoors at a pretty rapid clip, food trucks are still central. One of my favourites is *El Mar Azul* in Highland Park, which serves incredible Mexican seafood tostadas, with shrimp, octopus, crab and abalone in creamy slaw with hot sauce. From the new wave, *Guerrilla Tacos* and *Free Range* are worth it for creativity and flavor.

And for a quality dinner experience that wouldn't annihilate your wallet?

Elena's Greek-Armenian Cuisine is on LA's Middle Eastern Mount Rushmore, with some of the city's best kebabs, falafel, lentil soup, and stuffed grape leaves. In Koreatown I'm always happy to eat at *Soban*. Recently, I've been craving food from *Hatchet Hall*, a Southern restaurant with a wood grill and a seasonal California twist. *Cassia* is also fantastic, with some of the

most memorable Southeast Asian food outside of Southeast Asia.

Now—annihilate our wallets.

The quickest route is either omakase or kaiseki. *Urasawa* is out of range for a food writer, but maybe you have cash to spare. Down a notch is *N/naka*, Niki Nakayama's ambitious, seasonal restaurant in Palms, where she won't serve the same dish twice. *Nozawa Bar* and *Q* are standout omakase restaurants with the city's most pristine seafood. And steak fans try *Cut by Wolfgang Puck*, with a war chest of real-deal wagyu beef.

What about bars? Where for a good craft beer or a delicious cocktail?

We're lucky to live in a golden age for craft beer and cocktails in LA, and the scene's getting deeper by the month. *Beachwood BBQ & Brewing* in Long Beach is a favourite spot, since they brew some of the best beer in Cali, but also rotate serious guest kegs. For cocktails, hit any bar hosting a *Matt Biancaniello* pop-up, since his market-driven drinks are next level. Otherwise, grab a cocktail at *The Tasting Kitchen*.

Any tips on buying fresh produce?

Farmers' markets have fantastic produce and are also a great way to learn about seasonal produce. Santa Monica Market on Wednesdays and Hollywood Market on Sundays are particularly diverse.

And where to burn off the calories?

Westridge hiking trail is pretty central, not too steep, and culminates at a cool old radar station that supposedly protected us against Soviet missile attacks and now provides 360-degree views of the city. Plus Eagle Rock in the Santa Monica Mountains is pretty magical.

Angel's Share

Native Made

Sourced from all over the Southwest, these vintage Native American accessories are crafted from silver and turquoise, and each is one of a kind.
• Turquoise adornments, Honeywood, honeywoodvintage.com

The Rad Hatter

Stylish visitors come from all over the world to hatmaker Nick Fouquet's workshop in Venice. The unique handmade toppers are timeless investments, sure to elevate any lady or gentleman's wardrobe.
• Straw hat, Nick Fouquet, nickfouquet.com

Aromatic

A golden-age Hollywood starlet's dressing room is conjured by Goest Perfumes' "Silent Films". The moody scent is part of Jacqueline Steele's small collection of unisex fragrances, meant to work with one's own natural scent rather than cloak it.
• "Silent Films" Goest Perfumes, goest.us

Books

House of Leaves
• Mark Danielewski, 2000

This monster opus begins with the discovery of a text analysing a documentary that never existed. It tells of an LA family who find their house is expanding—on the inside. Borges meets Cortázar with shades of Foster Wallace—"HoL" is a baffling map of suburban insanity.

The Black Dahlia
• James Ellroy, 1987

Latter-day Los Angeles prophet Ellroy brings two fictional detectives to the true story of a 1940s murder in the first novel of his neo-noir "LA Quartet". He's described it as an attempt to come to terms with the murder of his own mother when he was ten years old.

Ask The Dust
• John Fante, 1939

Aspiring writer Arturo Bandini moons about LA dismayed by devastating poverty and orgiastic wealth in this era-defining novel. It was set for obscurity before its discovery in a public library by Charles Bukowski, who later proclaimed "Fante was my god".

Films

Los Angeles Plays Itself
• Thom Anderson, 2004

Based on his lectures exploring the portrayal of Los Angeles in cinema, Thom Anderson's documentary explores the way Hollywood has overshadowed LA, even blaming film for the name's abbrevation. A fascinating observation on the relationship between Los Angeles and its main industry.

The Player
• Robert Altman, 1992

Few things in film can be as refreshingly funny as when Hollywood mocks itself. Featuring a star-studded list of cameo appearances, Robert Altman's classic makes good use of Hollywood insider humour while offering up a biting critique of the power struggles at play in Tinseltown.

Annie Hall
• Woody Allen, 1977

Although mostly known for his depictions of Manhattan, Woody Allen serves one of the most biting critiques of Los Angeles' leading industry and lifestyle in "Annie Hall". When Annie proclaims LA as being "so clean", Allen counters: "That's because they don't throw their garbage away; they turn it in to television shows."

Music

Pet Sounds
• The Beach Boys, 1966

To call "Pet Sounds" an essential LA record is an understatement. And though it has the Beach Boys tag, this era-defining album is the epitome of Brian Wilson's emancipation from that outfit. Go for the stereo version on "The Pet Sounds Sessions".

The Chronic
• Dr. Dre, 1992

Featuring the beginnings of a beautiful relationship with Snoop Dogg, Dre's debut remains the quintessential hip hop oeuvre. Sixteen tracks of fat beats and sampled surprises—from Parliament-Funkadelic to Led Zeppelin—make it a no-brainer for true old-school LA.

Moving On
• Kan Wakan, 2014

LA trio Kan Wakan's sound is difficult to categorise, which might be just what they want. Nonetheless, "cinematic" would be a perfect way to describe their epic orchestral arrangements—ideal backdrop for Kristianne Bautista's moody vocals.

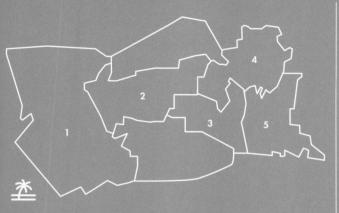

The Tasting Kitchen
1314 7th Street
+1 310-393-6699
cassiala.com
→ p.59 Ⓕ

Venice Beach Wines
529 Rose Avenue
+1 310-606-2529
venicebeachwines-hub.
com → p.23 Ⓝ

William Turner Gallery
2525 Michigan
Avenue E-1
+1 310-453-0909
williamturnergallery.
com → p.23 Ⓒ

2/Greater Hollywood

101 Coffee Shop
6145 Franklin Avenue
+1 323-467-1175
101coffeeshop.com
→ p.9 Ⓕ

American Rag Cie
150 South La Brea
Avenue
+1 323-935-3154
amrag.com → p.44 Ⓢ

Babylon
1320 Highland Avenue
+1 323-450-9584
babylon.la → p.44 Ⓢ

Canter's Deli
419 North Fairfax
Avenue
+1 323-651-2030
cantersdeli.com
→ p.23 Ⓕ

Chateau Marmont
8221 Sunset Boulevard
+1 323-656-1010
chateaumarmont.com
→ p.52 Ⓝ

Cinefamily at Silent Movie Theatre
611 North Fairfax
Avenue
+1 323-655-2510
cinefamily.org
→ p.32 Ⓒ

Cut
9500 Wilshire
Boulevard
+1 310-276-8500
fourseasons.com/
beverlywilshire/
dining/restaurants/cut
→ p.59 Ⓕ

El Carmen
8138 West 3rd Street
+1 323-852-1552
elcarmenla.net
→ p.44 Ⓕ

FourTwoFour on Fairfax
424 North Fairfax
Avenue
+1 323-424-4842
fourtwofouronfairfax.
com → p.44 Ⓢ

Freds
9570 Wilshire
Boulevard
+1 310-777-5877
barneys.co → p.23 Ⓕ

Gagosian Gallery
456 North
Camden Drive
+1 310-271-9400
gagosian.com
→ p.43 Ⓒ

Gallery 825
825 North La
Cienega Boulevard
+1 310-652-8272
gallery825.com
→ p.23 Ⓒ

H. Lorenzo
8660 Sunset Boulevard
+1 310-659-0058
hlorenzo.com
→ p.44 Ⓢ

Hollyhock House
4800 Hollywood
Boulevard
+1 323-913-4030
barnsdall.org/visit/
hollyhock-house
→ p.11 Ⓒ

Hollywood Market Wine & Food Store
1600 Ivar Avenue
+1 323-463-3171
seela.or → p.59 Ⓕ

Kohn Gallery
1227 Highland Avenue
+1 323-461-3311
kohngallery.com
→ p.23 Ⓒ

Los Angeles Municipal Art Gallery
4800 Hollywood
Boulevard
+1 323-644-6269
lamag.org → p.11 Ⓒ

Maude
212 South
Beverly Drive
+1 310-859-3418
mauderestaurant.com
→ p.11 Ⓕ

MiniBar
6141 Franklin Avenue
+1 323-798-4939
minibarhollywood.com
→ p.9 Ⓝ

Moran Bondaroff
937 North La Cienega
Boulevard
+1 310-652-1711
moranbondaroff.com
→ p.43 Ⓒ

Nozawa Bar
212 North Canon Drive
+1 424-216-6158
nozawabar.com
→ p.59 Ⓕ

Passport Harun Collective
310 North Stanley
Avenue
+1 323-913-4030
passportharun.com
→ p.44 Ⓢ

Regen Projects
6750 Santa Monica
Boulevard
+1 310-276-5424
regenprojects.com
→ p.22 Ⓒ

Sake House Miro
809 South La Brea
Avenue
+1 323-939-7075
sakehousemiro.com
→ p.44 Ⓕ

Santa Monica Market
5700 Santa Monica
Boulevard
+1 323-962-4474
→ p.59 Ⓕ

Soho House West Hollywood
9200 Sunset Boulevard
+1 310-432-9200
sohohousewh.com
→ p.54 Ⓝ

Stella McCartney
8823 Beverly Boule-
vard
+1 310-273-7051
stellamccartney.com
→ p.30 Ⓢ

Sundance Cinemas West Hollywood
8000 Sunset Boulevard
+1 323-654-2217
sundancecinemas.com
→ p.32 Ⓒ

Kohn Gallery
8071 Beverly
Boulevard
+1 323-658-8088
→ p.23 Ⓒ

The Polo Lounge
9641 Sunset Boulevard
+1 310-887-2777
dorchestercollection.
com → p.52 Ⓕ

The Virgil
4519 Santa Monica
Boulevard
+1 323-660-4540
thevirgil.com
→ p.59 Ⓝ

Upright Citizens Brigade Theatre
5919 Franklin Avenue
+1 323-908-8702
losangeles.ucbtheatre.
com → p.8 Ⓒ

Urasawa
218 North Rodeo Drive
+1 310-247-8939
→ p.59 Ⓕ

Virgil Normal
4157 Normal Avenue
+1 323-741-8489
virgilnormal.com
→ p.44 Ⓢ

Zinqué
8684 Melrose Avenue
+1 424-284-3930
lezinque.com
→ p.23 Ⓕ

3/Down-town

Ace Hotel
929 South Broadway
+1 213-623-3233
acehotel.com/
losangele → p.14 Ⓝ

Alchemy Works
826 East 3rd Street
+1 323-487-1497
alchemyworks.us
→ p.19 Ⓢ

4/Northeast

Honeywood
5117 York Boulevard
honeywoodvintage.
com → p.49, 60 Ⓢ

La Abeja
3700 North Figueroa
Street
+1 323-221-0474
laabeja.tumblr.com
→ p.15 Ⓕ

La Cuevita
5922 North
Figueroa Street
+1 323-255-6871
lacuevitabar.com
→ p.48 Ⓝ

Los Angeles Police
Museum
6045 York Boulevard
+1 323-344-9445
laphs.org → p.17 Ⓒ

Masa of Echo Park
Bakery & Cafe
1800 West Sunset
Boulevard
+1 213-989-1558
masaofechopark.com
→ p.15 Ⓕ

Metro Balderas
5305 North
Figueroa Street
+1 323-478-8383
→ p.48 Ⓕ

Mount Analog
5906 1/2 N
Figueroa Street
+1 323-474-6649
climbmountanalog.com
→ p.14 Ⓢ

My Taco
6300 York Blvd #4
+1 323-256-2698
my-taco.com
→ p.48 Ⓕ

Neutra VDL Studio
and Residences
2300 Silver Lake
Boulevard
neutra-vdl.org
→ p.46 Ⓒ

Otherwild Goods
& Services
1768 North Vermont
Avenue
+1 323-546-8437
otherwild.com
→ p.47 Ⓢ

Permanent Records
5116 York Boulevard
+1 323-739-6141
permanentrecordsla.
com → p.14 Ⓢ

Snivling Sibling
5028 North Eagle
Rock Boulevard
+1 323-344-0606
→ p.49 Ⓢ

Sunbeam Vintage
106 South Avenue 58
+1 323-908-9743
sunbeamvintage.com
→ p.49 Ⓢ

The Bearded Beagle
5926 North
Figueroa Street
+1 323-258-5898
thebeardedbeagle.com
→ p.49 Ⓢ

The Oinkster
2005 Colorado Blvd
+1 323-255-6465
theoinkster.com
→ p.48 Ⓢ

The Stash on York
6000 York Boulevard
+1 323-999-7474
stashonyork.com
→ p.49 Ⓢ

Trois Familia
3510 Sunset Boulevard
+1 323-725-7800
troisfamilia.com
→ p.47 Ⓕ

Urchin
5006 York Boulevard
+1 323-259-9059
→ p.49 Ⓢ

US Office Machine Co
5722 North Figueroa
Street
+1 323-256-2111
→ p.49 Ⓢ

Via-Mar
5111 North
Figueroa Street
+1 323-255-4929
→ p.15 Ⓕ

Weepah Way
5151 York Blvd
→ p.49 Ⓢ

Wombleton Records
5123 York Boulevard
+1 213-422-0069
wombletonrecords.com
→ p.14 Ⓢ

5/Eastside

Rosamund Felsen
Gallery
1923 South Santa
Fe Avenue #100
+1 310-828-8488
rosamundfelsen.com
→ p.23 Ⓒ

The Airliner
2419 North Broadway
+1 323-221-0771
→ p.14 Ⓝ

6/Other

Beachwood BBQ
& Brewing
210 E 3rd Street,
Long Beach
+1 562-436-4020
beachwoodbbq.com
→ p.59 Ⓕ

Bill's Burgers
14742 Oxnard Street,
Van Nuys
+1 818-785-4086
→ p.23 Ⓕ

Elena Greek-Armenian
Cuisine
1000 S Glendale
Avenue, Glendale
+1 818-241-5730
elenasgreek.com
→ p.59 Ⓕ

Huntington Library
& Gardens
1151 Oxford Road,
San Marino
+1 626-405-2100
huntington.org
→ p.30 Ⓞ

Malibu Farm Café
23000 Pacific Coast
Highway, Malibu
+1 310-456-1112
malibu-farm.com
→ p.52 Ⓕ

Nobu Malibu
22706 Pacific Coast
Highway, Malibu
+1 310-317-9140
noburestaurant.com
→ p.52 Ⓕ

Tacos Villa Corona
3185 Glendale
Boulevard, Glendale
+1 323-661-3458
→ p.23 Ⓕ

Available from LOST iN

Next Issue: Ibiza

Cartier

Matt Graham

Sometimes I can't sleep. I'll get up around 2 or 3am, dress in a good suit—a Varvatos, maybe—and before leaving the house I'll put on one of my five Cartier watches. I love Cartier. Their official promotional text says: "Cartier is a brand that projects luxury living from the outset." That's an image I'm proud to say I embrace. Then I'll get in the car. I'll check myself in the rear-view mirror, make sure I'm looking good, and I'll head to one of the bad parts of town, one of the areas someone driving a car like mine has no business going to. I have a police radio in my car, so I'll check in every once in a while, find out which area is a current crime hot spot, and that's where I'll go. I usually find a gas station or a strip mall, and park up where I'll be nice and visible. I want everyone around there to see me.

I mean, just one look at my car will tell you I don't belong there. You see, I'm a realtor, and being a realtor in LA is all about what you pull up in. I mean if you drive the wrong car in this town, people look at you like you're a piece of shit. I drive a Maserati Granturismo because I want people to know that I live the dream every day. It's an aggressive choice but I have a strong personal belief in honesty. I can spend about 45 minutes talking about my car with a client, that's how much I care about it: it isn't the horsepower or the speaker system, it's the feel and the spirit it projects that attracts me. It's the way people look at me when I get out. I smile and they know I'm going to sell them a house.
When my hand comes out for them to shake, it's got a Cartier like this one around the wrist. A Cartier watch says: I matter. In this world you're either a Winner or a Loser, and well, you can guess which I am.
But I'm getting off track. Don't let me. It's that personal belief in honesty of mine again getting me carried away. The watch is why I'm telling you this, because I'll have the same Cartier watch round my wrist when I get out of my car on the wrong side of town. I'll walk a few blocks, making sure everyone around there at that time of night gets a good, long look at my Cartier. Everyone wants what they don't have, and at some point someone will try to rob me.

That's when I bring my gun out.
At home I've got a cabinet with five guns. I've got a Glock, a Sig Sauer, a Ruger if I'm feeling like I really need to let off steam, a couple others.
These lowlifes will come at me one second, and the next they've got my Ruger in their faces and I'm telling them to suck on it if they want to live. They always run away, and the rush carries me all the way back to my bed in Orange County. You really ought to try it.
I started out on Skid Row just east of the nicer parts of Downtown LA where the expensive restaurants are, walking around the disgusting tent city where the homeless live, waiting for one of those Losers to try for my Cartier so I could give them a look at my gun.
Thing is, once you sell a million-dollar house, you start to think about selling a house that's worth three to five. After a while, those homeless guys were so pathetic,

they started to make me even feel sorry for them. I mean when someone's trying to rob you and you can smell their shit—I needed more of a challenge.

Now I mainly hit the 110, and head South, getting off the freeway around Florence or Gage Avenue, and drifting around the dark streets down there, finding a spot, parking up and then walking around till something happens.
So last week I run into this group of hardcore bangers before I even park, surrounding me. I just played dumb like I was some rich USC ex-fratboy douche bag lost in the wrong part of town. When I put my hands up, I made sure I let them get a good look at my Cartier just like I do when I sell a million-dollar house.
Next thing I know they're pulling a submachine gun on me, telling me to take the watch off my wrist, and then telling me I have to suck their dicks one after the other if I want to live. It was so perfect, because I played scared, pleading, getting out of the car. I told them I had money in the trunk, because I just sold a house up in the Hills for cash, so they let me open it...

And that's when I brought up my AK 47.
I said I had five guns. The AK's my favourite.
I took their weapons off them, told them to run. In the end, they were the ones got jacked, not me. Here's the funny part: some civilian filmed the whole thing. My AK in their faces, them backing away. You might have seen it on YouTube. Next thing you know, they're calling me an "urban hero." "Real estate agent turned hero vigilante" read one article, and now I'm at Café Gratitude telling a date about my car, or my personal belief in honesty, and people are coming up to me, telling me how I inspire them... and I'm selling more houses than ever.
And best of all, now in my cabinet, as well as the pistols and the AK, I've also got a Cobray M11 submachine gun, and a Mossberg pistol grip shotgun. They're all going to come in useful, because I'm stepping up my nightly excursions. I love LA.

Hey, you asked about my watch, buddy.

Screenwriter Matt Graham was born in London but has lived all over the world: Buenos Aires, New Orleans and the Amazon Rainforest, and is today a proud Angeleno. His writing work has most recently been seen on Showtime's hit popular documentary series "Oliver Stone's Untold History of the United States". He's also the author of a novel about a serial killer in the London rush hour, "The Night Driver", and a TV pilot about Dick Cheney so controversial no one has touched it... Yet

ON THE ROAD

The App for the Discerning Traveller

Explore insider recommendations and create your personal itinerary with handpicked locations tailored to your desires. Our selection of experiences ranges from independent boutiques, galleries, neighbourhood bars to brand new restaurants. Experience a new city from within.

LOST iN

REPLAY

PLACE STAMP
HERE

www.majawyh.com

www.replayjeans.com

REPLAY

PLACE STAMP
HERE

www.majawyh.com

www.replayjeans.com